Lawn Mower Chronicles

Lisa Head

Based on a True Story

ISBN-13:978-1477612644

ISBN-10:1477612645

Printed in the USA

DEDICATION

For my friends and family who shared in my
lawn mower drama, as it played out.

CONTENTS

ACKNOWLEDGMENTS

Author Photo by Abbi Enright

CHAPTER 1

Ain't I awesome?" yells my four year old son covered from head to toe with mud. He was awesome, except for the fact he was walking across my brand new carpet. It gave me the few seconds I needed to stop my 2-year-old from following the same trail to show me his awesome-ness. This thrilling story is just one of the many since moving into our new home in the summer of 2010. Along with the new home, came 5 acres of land that was formally a cornfield. When you move from a small house with a small yard, five-acres is massive.

My friends began telling me, "You need a garden tractor" to mow this massive property. So the search began. I had no idea what a roller coaster ride I was in for that summer and for summers to come.

My 2-year-old son's two favorite things to do are eating and taking a bath. It took only one time of using both in a sentence, to never do that again. I yelled for my boys, three in all, to "Come in and get ready to eat and take your bathes," In ran all three boys. However, my two-year-old began undressing at the door, including his diaper and made a beeline to the tub completely undressed. He was ready to hop into the tub at that very moment. I yelled, "Whoa, you have to eat first," so back to the table he headed and down he plopped at the table to eat. It had all the makings of one of those "Kodak Moments."

Along with all the fun we were having, I

was faced with the care and maintenance of my newly acquired 5 acres of land. So, off I went looking for a riding mower. Up to this point of my life I had only used push mowers. It was obvious, even to me, that this yard could not be mowed with a push mower. The first summer was dry and the only grass I had was where the landscaper had planted grass. The rest of the property was the remains of corn stalks and weeds. And I don't mean just regular old weeds, but weeds that were up to 7 foot tall. It was great for the kids to hide in, but it was not a pretty sight. We were not in any danger of Homes and Gardens stopping by to take pictures.

Time to tackle the purchase of a riding lawn tractor. Boy oh boy, I didn't have any idea of what was in store for me. I looked through sale flyers, searched the Internet, and visited local stores for a mower that would be right for me and that I could afford.

Being the single mother of three small boys didn't make my search any easier. For some reason, my boys thought I should choose a lawn tractor by color, red in particular, rather than by reputation. As I look back, their method worked as well, if not better, than mine did. The search had begun and I was honing in on a lawn tractor.

I dragged my boys around as we went from town to town to look at used lawn tractors. It was not out of the question for us to drive over an hour to look at a tractor, standing in the pouring rain, and being shown a tractor that was being held together with gray tape. Granted, I understand that in Midwest gray tape is considered the fix all, but it was not in me to spend hundreds of dollars for a tractor whose original color was unrecognizable. With gasoline being priced at close to $3 a gallon, my method of covering the countryside to save money was costing me more money than just buying a new lawn tractor. So, that is what I decided to do, buy new, can't make a mistake there, I thought, and boy was I ever wrong using that theory!

Now it is important to understand that I was driving around in a mini-van with three kids all of who were still in car seats. When I, if I ever did, figure out what lawn tractor to buy, I would have a whole new set of issues to solve. How would I get it home? Where would I keep it stored? Did I need attachments? Who would put on these attachments? Would I be able to change any of these attachments myself? The one thing I did know was that I wanted it to double as a snow plow/thrower for my new 80-foot driveway. Knowing that living in the middle of a cornfield means no wind breaks. I lived close to work, but if I couldn't get out of my drive, that didn't matter much.

I was most definitely playing Beat the

Clock, with the weeds getting higher by the day. It was time to make a decision, to bite the bullet, and pick out a lawn tractor and get to the business of cleaning up my new homestead. Off to the dealer we went to buy a brand new lawn tractor. I remember that day, oh so clearly, having no idea what was ahead of me. I picked out a 42" deck lawn tractor. Paying for it with half in cash and the other half with a check, I was ready to get to work. At this point, we were still living at our old house. Moving day was set to take place in a few weeks.

Now I had to figure out how I was going to get it home. Good news, I could pay $50 and they would deliver it to me. Then I needed to decide if I wanted it delivered to new house or the old one. I opted for old, so that I wouldn't have to worry about someone stealing the mower. Not knowing that might have saved me way too many headaches. I should have known when the mower only came with enough gas to get it started and off the trailer, that this lawn tractor and I were not going to get along. Just for the record, this lawn tractor was yellow, much to the boys' disappointment.

CHAPTER 2

The lawn tractor arrived and was parked next to the driveway. The boys had a great time climbing up on it and posing for pictures. The boys were cute, however the lawn tractor wasn't. Since it was at my old house, I thought it would be a perfect opportunity to not only mow my lawn in a fraction of the time, but also my dad's yard. He lived two-doors down from me. I began mowing and everything was going great. I managed to mow my yard in about fifteen minutes and moved on over to my dad's house. There is when I received the first sign this was not the lawn tractor for me, but I am stubborn so I keep plugging away.

My dad was out in his yard working, so I started mowing outside the fence. Things were going great, I was a mean grass-cutting machine, and then it started. I stopped the mower to get off and moved a sign. I climbed back on and turned the key, silence, turned it again and nothing. My dad walked over and with me on it, he rocked the mower. I tried again and it fired right up. I chose to pretend it was just a freak thing, but pretending would get me nowhere.

Before moving day, we all headed over to the new house, minus the lawn tractor. The ground was still pretty torn up and wet, so at that point mowing wasn't an issue. My four-year old son ran around the back of the house. After a few minutes, I heard screams coming from the backyard. I ran around the corner to find him stuck in the mud up to his mid-calves. He wasn't going anywhere.

After I finished laughing, I found some boards to throw across the mud, walked over to him, and pulled him out, minus his shoes. It was doubtful we would ever see those shoes again.

Finally moving day was here. The seed for the grass had been sown and the weeds were even taller yet. The lawn tractor made it to its new home and sat, waiting to be used. I used it a few times to mow paths for the kids to use. I even mowed out a maze for them to play in, the weeds were that tall. Kids thought it was great, I thought it looked awful. During those few times I mowed, it stopped running about three different times. It was picked up and dropped back off several times, fixed. Later this would turn out to be a good thing, because when they fix a mower that is under warranty, the serial number is needed every time it goes in for repair.

That autumn I ended up having a friend come over with a bush hog to get rid of my weeds. This was a great disappointment to my children, because they could no longer get "lost" in the weeds. Another friend took off the mower deck and put on the snow blower; I never was able to get it started. So all winter it just sat in the garage.

Spring soon arrived and we changed the snow blower with the mowing deck. It started now and I thought I was back in business. Maybe, if I could keep them cut down, weeds wouldn't be an issue anymore. Not so, but doesn't hurt to dream.

CHAPTER 3

Everyone that has a lawn to mow knows that there are steps involved in preparing and then actually mowing the lawn. These might include checking the oil, putting in the gas, cleaning up clutter in the yard, starting it up and actually mowing the lawn. These should be the basic steps to mowing, but not the case with my lawn tractors.

Thanks to the wonderful world of the social networking, I was able to share my mower saga with all my friends and family. As time passed, I was able to finally get out there and start mowing.

It was wonderful, I would put my

earphones on, turned up the music, start up my mower and enter a world of peace. Then just a few feet from where my "me time" began the mower stopped cutting grass. The motor still worked, the deck was engaged, but nothing was coming out the mower deck. In the beginning, I would have to drive back to the house and fix the mower.

I posted the steps that were involved for me to mow my lawn.

Step 1: I would mow for a short while.

Step 2: I would drive the mower back to the house.

Step 3: I would try to fix the mower.

Step 4: I would rest due to the frustration brought on by the mower not working.

Step 5: I would go back outside and with a much clearer mind, I would fix the mower.

Step 6: I after I would put the belt back on the mower, I would start mowing once again.

Step 7: REPEAT STEPS 1-6. It was amazing how many of my friends and similar steps to their lawn mowing regiment.

My friend Lee added a few additional steps of his own.

Step 6: Determine starter is bad, order new gear.

Step 7: Discover gear cannot be ordered alone, have to order whole new starter.

Step 8: Starter has to be back ordered.

Step 9: Starter finally arrives.

Step 10: No gear on starter.

Step 11: Return starter, explaining the gear is missing.

Step 12: Discover gear can be ordered separately, but the clerk didn't know.

Step 13: New gear arrives, wrong size.

Step 14: Return gear, order correct size.

Step 15: Gear miss-ordered, new starter is sent, but with no gear.

Step 16: To Be Determined.

Not to be out done, Jake added just a few more steps to mowing. He too had his own mower issues.

Step 1: Buy New battery, starter and PTO belt.

Step 2: Purchase spacer and pin to hold the PTO belt. Goal: Get in two consecutive mows!

However, the overwhelming cry from my friends was to buy livestock. There was a difference in opinion as to which animal would best serve my needs. Goats were suggested, but it was decided that they would cause me to lose money.

According to my friend Bambi, "Goats tend to just eat and poop." Then the movement of finding the perfect addition to the homestead was moved to my purchasing sheep or Alpacas. This was felt to be a better solution, because, according to Bambi, they not only eat and poop, they also have wool that can be sheered, and I might have an opportunity to break even. I am still waiting for a barn raising party. So that we would have a place to keep all this livestock my friends were planning on me to buy.

Lisa Head

CHAPTER 4

The belt of my lawn tractor fell off so often that after a while I could replace the slipped belt, without getting off the mower. It was not out of the question to spend over six hours to mow my property. And it was a long rough ride. Finally, I lost my patience and took the mower apart. That is when I posted, "Fight with lawn mower...mower 1- me 0, but at least I am not in pieces all over the yard right now!"

While I was cooling off, a friend was looking on line for ideas on how to fix the problems I was having. What we did learn was that I was not alone in the fight against this machine. But as long as it was apart, that was the time to make some repairs. We were able to get hold of a diagram on what the belt system was supposed to look like. I also took that opportunity to change the blades. I adjusted the tension on the belt and then put the deck back on the mower. At this point, I declared victory over the mower, but it would be a short victory.

When looking at how the mower was supposed to be put together, my friend and I noticed we had an extra spring that was not attached to anything. When I posted victory Steve asked, "Did you get the deck back on and how about the errant spring?"

I replied with, "Yes, I did get the deck back. However, the hole that the spring was meant go in on the other side doesn't exist. So I drilled a hole for the spring. I put the bar that keeps the belt on, in the front, on backwards and the belt fell off. I will fix that tomorrow. Otherwise, the belt stayed in place for the entire two hours that I mowed. It does seem to be running better." The post took a short turn to vacuum cleaners, but quickly returned to mowers. Kicking and hitting of the mower were the suggestions that came next.

For the time being, I had a mower that would not only run, but also the belt would stay on too. I was back to mowing and having a bit of "me time." I was happy. Until I took it out one night to mow, after my kids went to bed. After all, isn't that the reason they sell them with headlights?

CHAPTER 5

After I put the boys to bed, I headed outside to mow. It was a lovely evening and I was enjoying my music, things were going well. I started working of the back half of my 5 acres, trying to be a good neighbor and make it look nicer all around. The weeds were high and I was really hoping that there would be no breakdowns, mostly because I was afraid of snakes.

I made a few rounds and things were going well. Then all of a sudden I heard a loud boom and smoke started rolling from the engine. I turned it off in a hurry and jumped off the mower. After the original smoke cleared, I could see that it was not on fire. I climbed back up, attempted to start the mower once again, I turned the key, and there was nothing, not a sound to be heard. There I was, trying to decide if I was going to sit on the mower until morning or hurry back to the house and hope there were no snakes on the way.

Then I tried the headlights. Yay, they worked and put off enough light that I could see. Apparently, the problem was not the battery. I began pushing the mower toward the house, watching for snakes the entire way. Finally, I reached the area that had already been mowed. I felt safe leaving the mower there and going to the house.

Once in the house, I began posting more about my mower saga and the response was great. I had declared that the war was over and the mower had won. After a long battle, I admitted defeat that night.

Again there was an outcry for sheep. My

friends and family on the social network, felt once again, that livestock was my best option. In all honesty, at this point I was in agreement. Livestock seemed to be the best option for my lawn care, or at least less trouble.

In reply, I wrote, "If it wasn't such a big mower, I would dig a hole and bury it! The weeds in the back are over my head. The USDA was going to plant trees, but ran out of money before they could. I was trying to get weeds down to give spontaneous trees a chance to suck up any rain we might get in the next few days." It had been a hot dry summer, but I knew the weeds would choke out any young saplings. I really was trying to help.

On the post, I agreed to buy sheep, mostly because they could walk themselves back to the house. Another friend, Tab, decided that, "Goats = lawn mower in the summer and food in the winter."

Yet in reply another friend posted, "Lamb tastes better than goat!"

Then the mood changed to that of condolences, sort of, with Julie writing, "Awe man, what a bummer! So sorry! The goat idea's not a bad one."

But the best came from my neighbor, Maggie, who was driving down her driveway that lines one side of my property. She commented on my post the next morning, "That is so funny because I was driving down the lane last night and I saw what looked like a white sheet moving on the east-side of your property. I couldn't figure out what it could be and I almost ran into a pole. It was you on your mower. I told my husband Aaron and he just about died laughing... Sorry about your mower though (Brush Hog anyone)!" I joking figured that at least I could make others happy with my misfortune.

Then came the icing on the proverbial cake. The boys and I got up early the next morning and left the house for a taekwondo class we all attend. We came home about lunchtime and I could see the mower sitting dead in my backyard. I thought about all the trouble and time it had caused me, how it had never made it through a complete mow and how much time I had spent repairing it.

After lunch I decided to walk out there and give it one more chance. It still wouldn't start, so I lifted the hood, and it wasn't all black and chard, which gave me a little hope. I crawled under the tractor and found the problem, time to celebrate, the drive shaft belt had broken. Manageable I figured, especially with all the experience I now had with belts. So, I loaded my boys into the van and we were off to buy a drive shaft belt.

CHAPTER 6

We were at the store for about 20 minutes; so with drive time we were gone a total of 45 minutes. I bought the belt, put the boys back in the van, drove home, and pulled into the driveway ready to tackle my mower once again. But it was not to be. When we pulled into the driveway, I opened the garage door, and I realized in a moment that we had been burglarized. The mower had been stolen, along with a few other things. There I stood new belt in hand, with no mower to put it on. Both the police and the community guessed that the burglars had been watching from the cornfield and saw us leave and then return.

Earlier in the summer, my dad built a frame around the top of the mower for covering. He used PVC pipe and screwed them on the frame to of the mower. It was not hard to remove; just a few screws and the frame would come off of the mower, no problem. But that was not an issue anymore, my next mission was to find a new mower.

Would the second one be better than the first one? I certainly didn't was to make the same mistake twice.

Back to searching for the mower of my dreams. I once again looked toward the social networks to help guide me in my decision making. The one thing about my friends is that they don't hold back when it comes to sharing an option.

My post for this particular search was, "Looking for a Good, Dependable and Inexpensive Riding Lawn Tractor, if anyone has suggestions or knows of one for sale, please let me know." The response was unexpected. Now they went from livestock to a live man. There was a great debate as to whether or not I needed a man to help.

The comments went from Tab stating, "What is the maximum of your definition of "inexpensive"?

I responded with, "Depends, all my lawn equipment, tools, golf clubs, fishing poles and more were stolen last week and I need to replace much of it in order to do what needs to be done around here. Waiting on the insurance to help, meanwhile the grass and weeds continue to grow."

Apparently, Tab had not been keeping up with my posts and was totally unaware we had been burglarized. So to my post, he responded, "Stole from your house?" That was the point the links started coming. From as far as Texas, Tab and I went on a search for a good mower. He would send me links and I would check them out. However, I had to wait for insurance money to come in from the burglary to have enough to buy a mower. For a few weeks, there was no mowing at my house.

Another friend, Karen, felt that I should have capitalized DEPENDABLE. I would have to agree with her on that one.

As they moved towards the topic of my finding a mate, the response was varied. My friend Milly commented "My saying when I was young, was that I was looking for a man with a riding lawn mower and group insurance, but I never found him," with a smile.

In response to that comment, Tab posted, "OR you can find a decent man with great advice on-line. Without any of the hassles of having a stupid man around:)" The jury is still out as to whether or not I could fix this problem with a man.

Oh happy day, so I thought. I found a great deal on a lawn tractor. I drove to the

nearest town to purchase an upscale mower
that had been returned. I was assured that it
would be fine, because the previous owner
had put too much oil in it and all the
company had to do was clean out the oil and
start over. It was a great deal; they would
have to sell it to me at a reduced cost
because it was used, but was "just like new."
I loaded up the kids, the lawn tractor, and
full of hope for a better mowing, I headed
home.

Lisa Head

CHAPTER 7

I was soon on-line sharing my hope for the future with my latest mower. I shared with Tab that, "I picked one up. The one we talked about in chat was there, but they had one that was a step higher and cheaper due to being refurbished. I have used it on my front lawn this evening and it cuts beautifully...."

To this Tab replied, "Upgrade + cheaper =deal! Did you get the warranty also?" To which I was able to answer yes, at least a 30-day warranty. But it wouldn't take 30 days to find out this was not the mower for me. This chapter deals with the four, yes I said four, days I had my second mower. On the second day I was posting, "ARGGGGGG! If I weren't a "nice" person, I would really be burning up (social network) right now! HINT: Has to do with Lawn Tractor's!"

The comment that followed, "You sure have a love-hate relationship with tractors, more hate than love, I hope it gets better."

Out of patience, I replied, "You have that right, the kicker is that I could have fixed it myself IF SOMEONE HADN'T STOLEN MY TOOLS!

Bought extended warranty, but they are not sure it covers the problems I am having. They assured me I did have 30 days to return the tractor. You might be seeing us heading up the road sooner rather than later! Are there any lawn tractors that are any good?"

Tab posted, "What the heck happened? IF you got the warranty it's good for one FREE replacement, but I don't know how that applies to a refurbished mower."

I commented back to Tab with, "I

bottomed out in mud and the blade bent to a 90 degree angle, but they are sure it was something I did. I told them that if the blades were that delicate I didn't want it anyway and returned it for a full refund!"

Now it was time to get serious, no more horsing around. I got on-line and started searching for the best lawn tractor made. Money was not an issue this time, I wanted to mow free of repairs, and also wanted something I could plow snow from my driveway in the winter. I meant business.

Then, at last, I think I have found the mower for me. Good name, good consumer rating and available nearby. I found a store on-line where I could purchase the snow blade; soon I would be back in business. This lead to my post, "Hoping 3rd time is the charm in the continuing mower saga! The story continues!"

Tab, however, just couldn't leave it alone and commented, "OK, I'm going there...

women drivers!"

It was at this point the topic of this book came up in the comments and posts directed toward me. Bambi felt I should write a book.

So when another friend, Karen, brought it up again, I commented, "Well Karen, Bambi thinks I have enough material for a book. Maybe this will be the final chapter! Down the road, when this all becomes a funny, a "Hey, do you remember that time," moment!"

To this Karen replied, "I agree with Bambi! You definitely have the material for a book! Go for it!

Tab's comment to the book was less than flattering, but very funny, "But then you'd just run over it too and ruin your next mower.

CHAPTER 8

I bought my new mower, the third one in a year, and brought it home. And I mowed without any problems; I was feeling great about my purchase. Maybe I had found the mower meant for me.

One beautiful summer's day, I walked out to get my mail. In my pile of mail was an official letter from the prosecutor's office. It appeared that our thieves had been arrested and were in jail. The notice also stated that some of my belongs may have been recovered. That same afternoon I received a phone call from the officer that had filled out my police report when we were burglarized. He called to inform me that my mower had been recovered and that I could probably get it back, if I made a deal with the insurance company to buy it back from them. This mower was like a bad penny; it just kept turning up.

After I explained to the officer that I had already replaced the mower and didn't want it back, he checked to see if any of my other things had been recovered. No, was the answer to that question.

A few days went by and the officer called again about the mower. Once again I explained that I didn't want the mower anymore, the insurance company could have it, with my blessings. At this point, he explained to me that they were able to find and arrest the person that had been fencing the stolen property. It seems an officer, in another town, was aware of the description of my stolen mower, yellow, "brand name," and the white frame that was attached to the mower. As he was driving down the road, he saw it parked in front of a business. He got out of his car, walked over to the mower, and checked the serial number it was a match. He then arrested the person inside. It would seem that my first mower's purpose on this earth was not to cut grass, but rather to catch bad guys.

Thanks to my mower, the leader of the burglary ring had been caught. Even though my mower was now a hero, I still didn't want it back.

Winter was soon here and we had taken off the mower deck of the third lawn tractor and put on a snow blade. Fortunately, it was a mild winter. The few times it did snow enough to warrant my getting out the tractor with the snow blade, I was thrilled each time it started. I was the happy owner of a lawn tractor/snow removal machine.

During the first snow, I realized that I really needed

chains for my back tires. My tractor's tires would just spin as I tried to push the snow.

I had an idea. I would back up the tractor as far as I could and then gun it into the snow banks. It worked most of the time. After the past year and a half, I considered this minor.

In Indiana we usually don't have to mow until May, but with the mild winter the grass grew quickly and early. By March the lawns were looking green and the grass was growing quickly. It was time to mow, so I removed the snow blade and attached the mower deck to the tractor. I was ready to mow.

CHAPTER 9

Happy about having a mower that worked and in joking about mowing so early in the year, I posted, "Reasons for not mowing:

1) it's too wet.

2) I don't have time right now.

3) It's too hot, grass will burn if it's cut

4) "Ozone Day", can't. In my case, you may add the following:

5) the belt fell off

6) the motor blow up and

7) my mower was stolen.

NEW FOR 2012:

8) it's ONLY March.

9) I can't afford the gas to put in my

mower. Welcome To Spring! It is a Beautiful Day!"

I was so happy with my mower. I even posted that I had mowed the entire property, twice without any breakdowns. My friends were in shock, but celebrated with me.

Then the real fun started. I got a flat tire, but that's okay, I can handle a flat tire. I tried to air it up and repair it, but no luck. Off to the store again, for a new tire. The mower was still at our house when we returned home. The tire came with adapters and I proceeded to replace the tire, using the adapters. The wheel wobbled when I drove, but it worked. I proceeded to mow.

Then on April 1, of all days, I had to post, "Not an April fool's joke...the TIRE fell off my mower! Someday this too will be funny. But today is not that day! Have at it all my 'social network' mower buddies from last year!" And they did.

Trina posted, "You and your lawn mower! I

had a friend (RIP) that had so much trouble with a lawn mower that he finally took a baseball bat to it! It showed it who was boss."

Julie wrote, "Aww Lisa! I feel horrible for chuckling because it really isn't funny! I just cannot believe your horrible luck with mowers!

I replied back with, "Don't feel bad Julie. If I didn't laugh I think my head might explode! It runs fine, but the wheel falls off when I drive it. It is pretty funny...just going to have to figure out a way to keep the wheel on, as long as it is still here tomorrow. I am done for today! Trina I just might go with the baseball bat idea!"

Another friend posted, "Lisa that seriously sounds like our mower saga last year. And yes it's funny now but we were so frustrated at the time. Hope you get it figured out!"

I made the final comment to this post, "I got the wheel to stay on long enough to get it to the garage, didn't want a repeat of last year (stolen). So the boys and I worked hard and it is safe and sound! We have lived in this house for two years and this is my third lawn tractor.

CHAPTER 10

The next day, I got the tire back on and it was working. It was still wobbling, but it was working. I had figured out why it fell off, so I was able to fix it. A couple of days later I went out to mow and there was a flat tire on the other side. I took it off and headed to the supply store again. They aired it up and no more problems. Back to mowing happily.

Headed out to mow just a few days ago, as I write this, and was able to finish about half of the property before it stopped running while engaged. So, once again I drove it back to the house to see if I could fix it this time too.

No matter what I tried, the mower would die every time the blades where engaged. It was late in the day, so I decided to park it in the garage and face it the next day. My post that night went,

"My love affair with my mower has come to a bitter end."

To which Trina replied, "Well now that is shocking!"

I took the mower out to the yard and removed the mower deck. While trying to pull it out from under the tractor, I got it wedged and I couldn't get it to budge. I push it, I pulled it, and I even kicked it, but it just sat there. Finally, I turned on the tractor and moved it slightly. It was enough to free the deck. I pulled out the mower deck and turned it over. After cleaning the dirt away, I discovered that the shaft that holds one of the blades on the mower had broken completely off. I took it off the deck and tried to decide what to do about it.

To Trina's 'shocking' comment, I replied, "Funny...NOT! Broke the deck holding one of the three blades. Got it off, but I don't know if I can replace it or not. ARGGGGGG!"

I put the broken piece of the mower and the attached blade in the trunk of my car. The next day we went looking for the part we needed. Found that the part could be ordered, but would take a couple of days. I ordered the part and when I went to pick it up, the repairman showed me where another section on the same piece was also bad. With this, I bought an entire new part, along with three new blades and headed home. The deck was still in the yard and the tractor was in the garage.

I flipped over the mower deck and proceeded to repair the broken part and replace all three blades. I noticed that the belt is very worn and I could see where the blade shaft was about to go on another blade, but pretended I didn't notice. I put the deck back together and was ready to attach it to the tractor. But when I walked into the garage, the wobbly tire was flat and could not be aired up. I took off the good tire to make sure I bought the correct tire this time, and headed to the supply store. I purchased a new tire, with adapters, and went back home to put it on the tractor. This time it came with directions and I was able to replace the wobbly tire with one that doesn't wobble.

I drove the tractor out to the mower deck and proceeded to put it back together. I turned it on, engaged the blades and it not only ran, it cut grass. I started mowing. About twenty minutes into mowing the lawn tractor began to shake, but I continued to mow.

I am still mowing; pretending there is nothing wrong. However I am in the market for an inexpensive, used farm tractor and a bush hog.

Stay Tuned

ABOUT THE AUTHOR

Lisa Head is an elementary music teacher and is a foster/adoptive parent. She has fostered children for several years. She has taught music for several years in a nearby public school system. Lisa has cared for and worked with many traditional and therapeutic children throughout the years.

Other writings of Lisa Head include: *Calbert: The Third-Grade Cowboy: Facing the Bully Nightmares and Ivory* (Working title) due out Feb. 2013

For more information visit us online.

www.authorlisahead.com

Made in the USA
Monee, IL
24 October 2021